Bond Assessment Papers

Second Papers in Non-verbal Reasoning

Andrew Baines

Paper 1

Which is the odd one out? Circle the letter.

Example

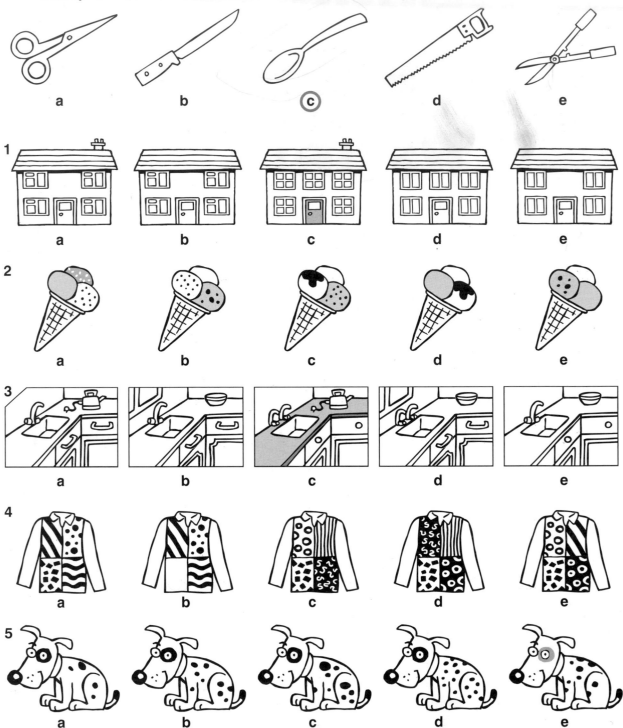

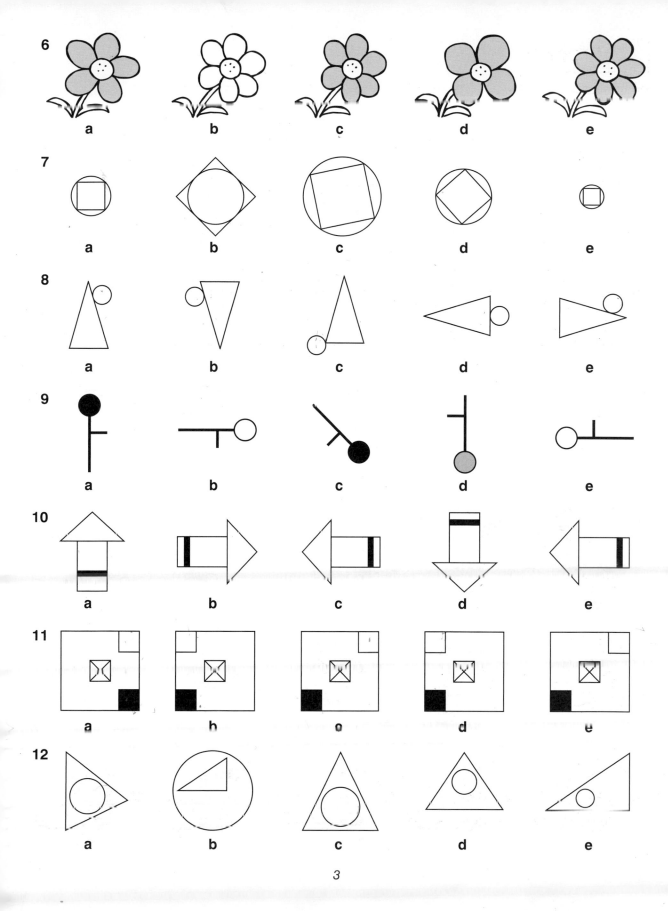

6
a   b   c   d   e

7
a   b   c   d   e

8
a   b   c   d   e

9
a   b   c   d   e

10
a   b   c   d   e

11
a   b   c   d   e

12
a   b   c   d   e

Which one comes next? Circle the letter.

Example

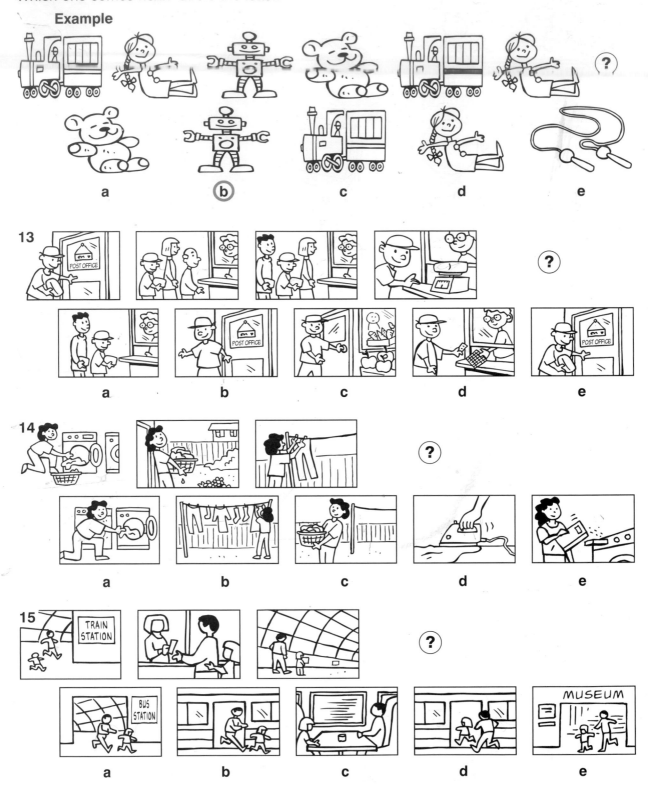

13

a   b   c   d   e

14

a   b   c   d   e

15

a   b   c   d   e

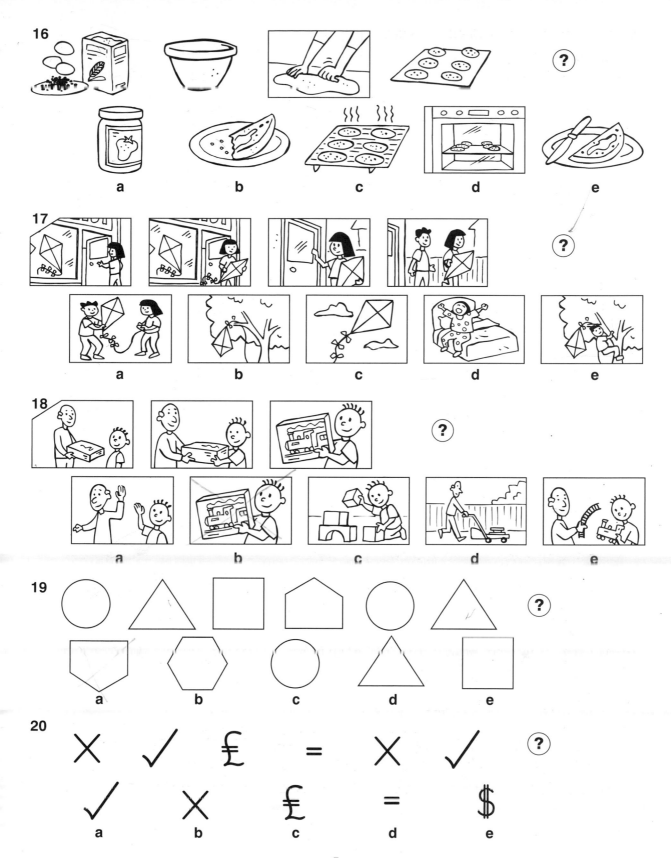

16

a b c d e

17

a b c d e

18

a b c d e

19

a b c d e

20

a b c d e

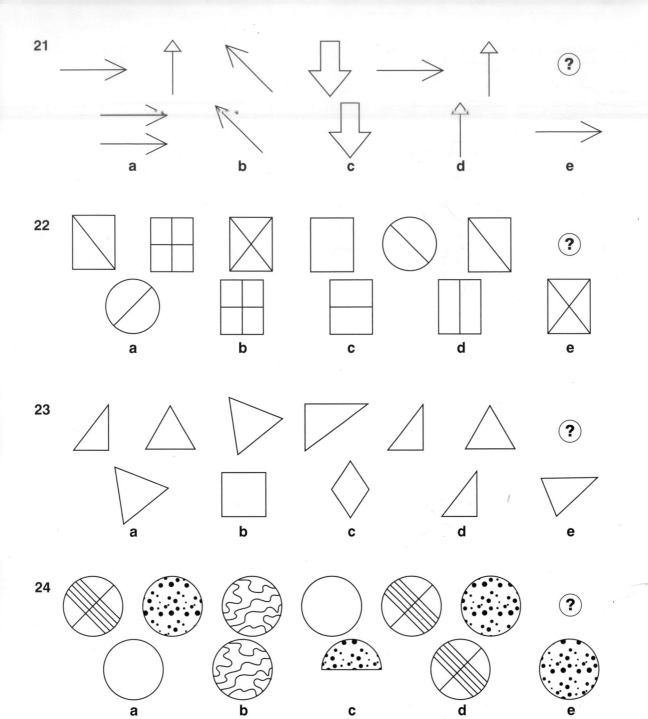

21

a b c d e

22

a b c d e

23

a b c d e

24

a b c d e

Choose the picture which completes the second pair in the same way as the first pair.
Circle the letter.

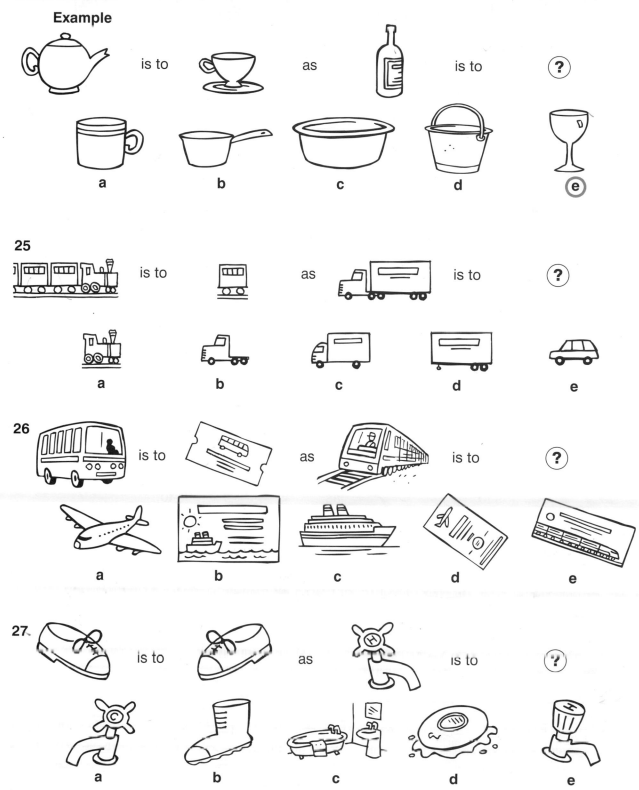

Example

25

26

27

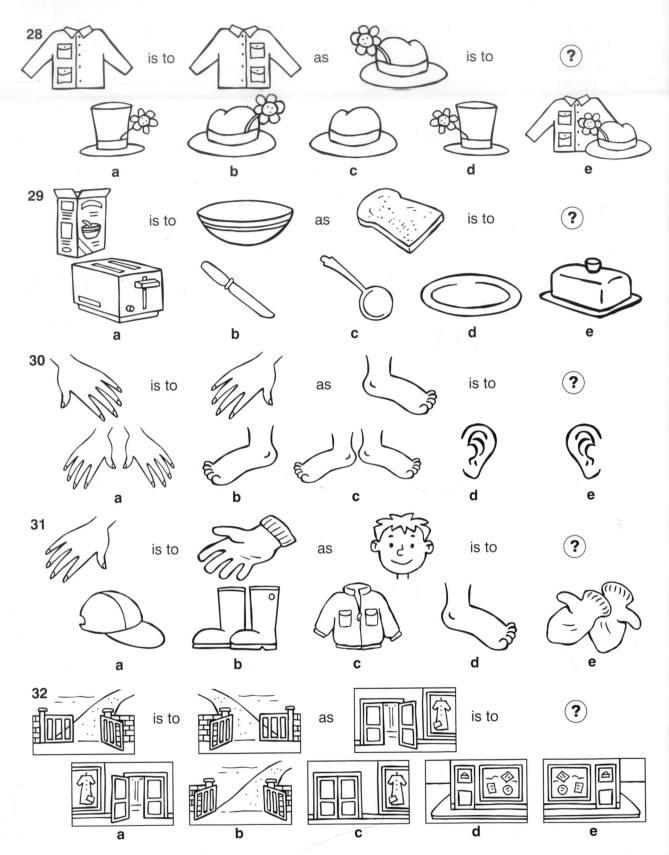

28 is to as is to ?

a b c d e

29 is to as is to ?

a b c d e

30 is to as is to ?

a b c d e

31 is to as is to ?

a b c d e

32 is to as is to ?

a b c d e

33

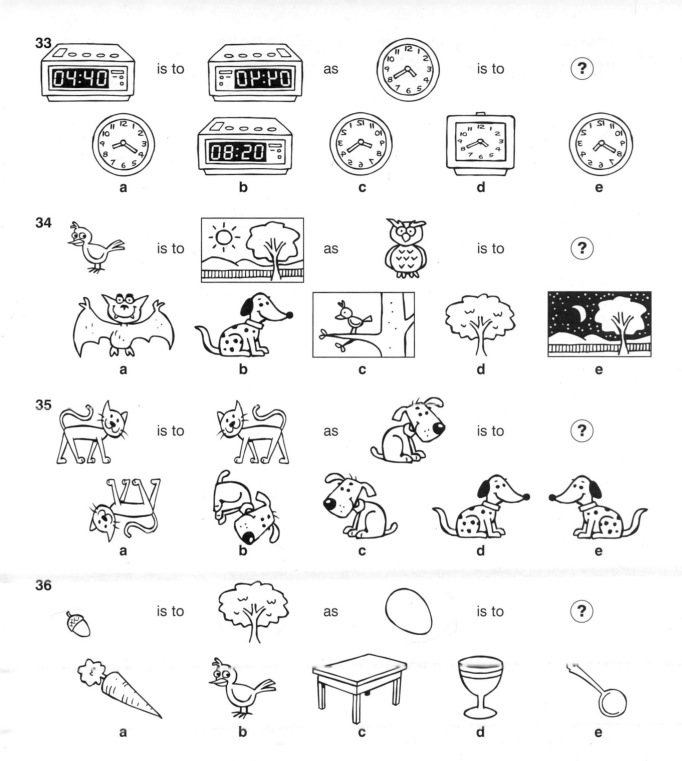

is to ... as ... is to ?

a   b   c   d   e

34

is to ... as ... is to ?

a   b   c   d   e

35

is to ... as ... is to ?

a   b   c   d   e

36

is to ... as ... is to ?

a   b   c   d   e

In which larger picture is the smaller picture hidden? Circle the letter.

Example

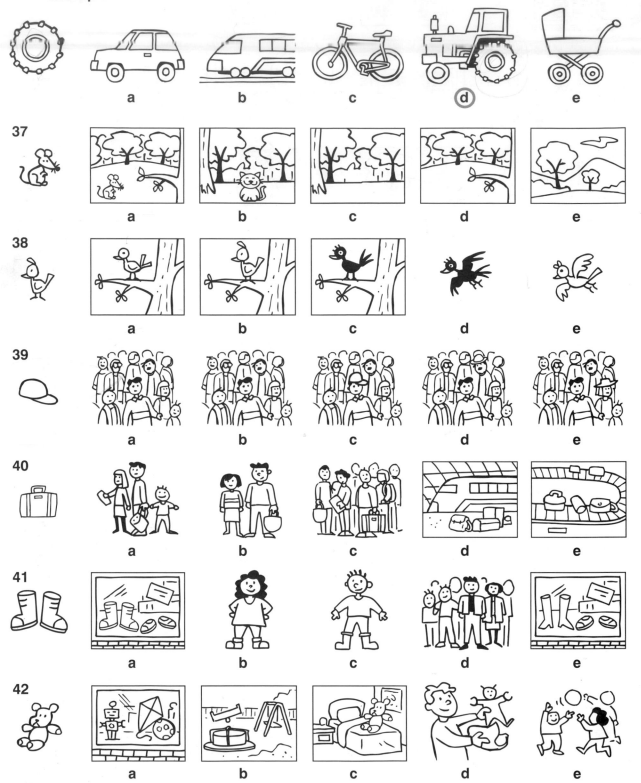

a   b   c   d   e

37

38

39

40

41

42

Choose the picture or shape which completes the larger square. Circle the letter.

Example

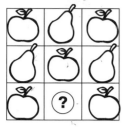

a   b   ©   d   e

43

a   b   c   d   e

44

a   b   c   d   e

45

a   b   c   d   c

46

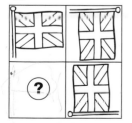

a   b   c   d   e

47

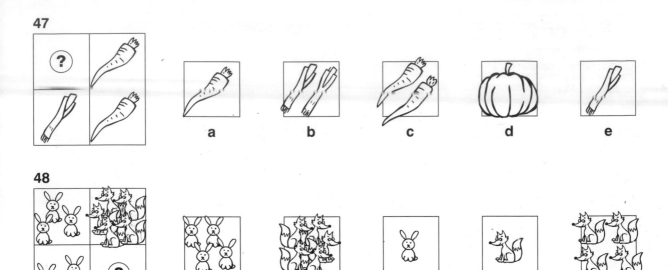

a   b   c   d   e

48

a   b   c   d   e

Paper 2

Which is the odd one out? Circle the letter.

Example

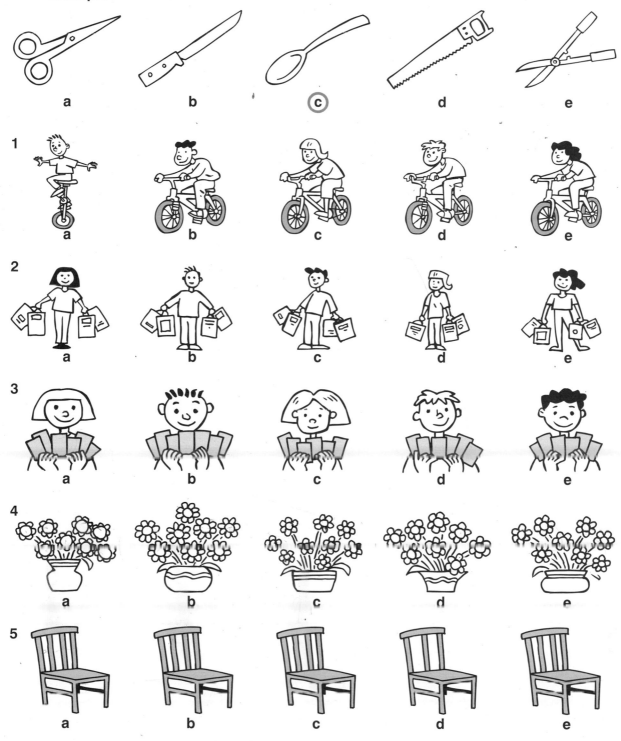

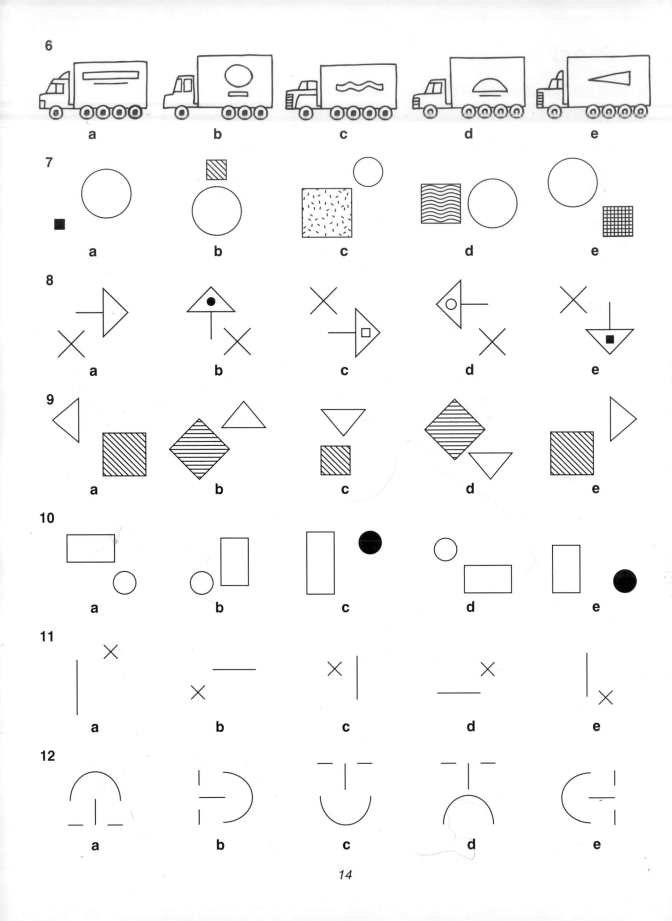

6

a   b   c   d   e

7

a   b   c   d   e

8

a   b   c   d   e

9

a   b   c   d   e

10

a   b   c   d   e

11

a   b   c   d   e

12

a   b   c   d   e

Which one comes next? Circle the letter.

Example

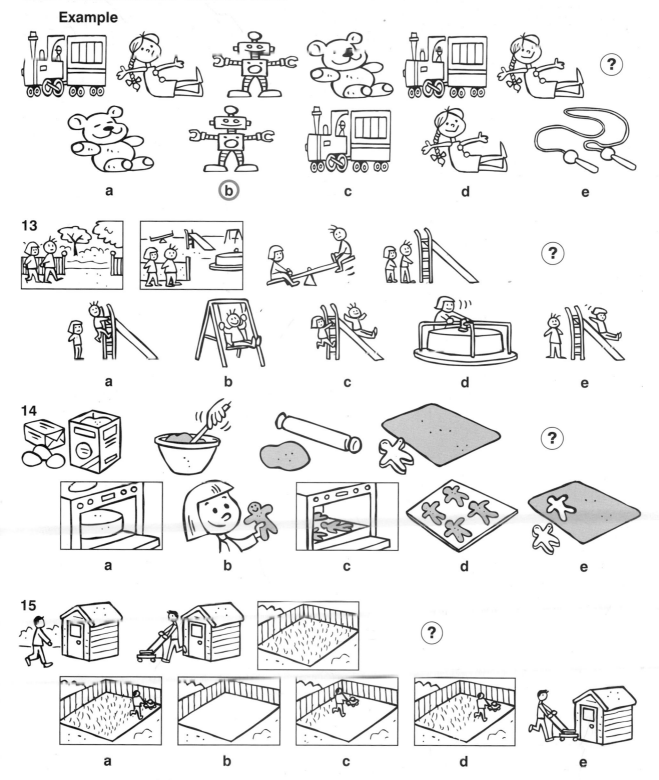

a   b   c   d   e

13

a   b   c   d   e

14

a   b   c   d   e

15

a   b   c   d   e

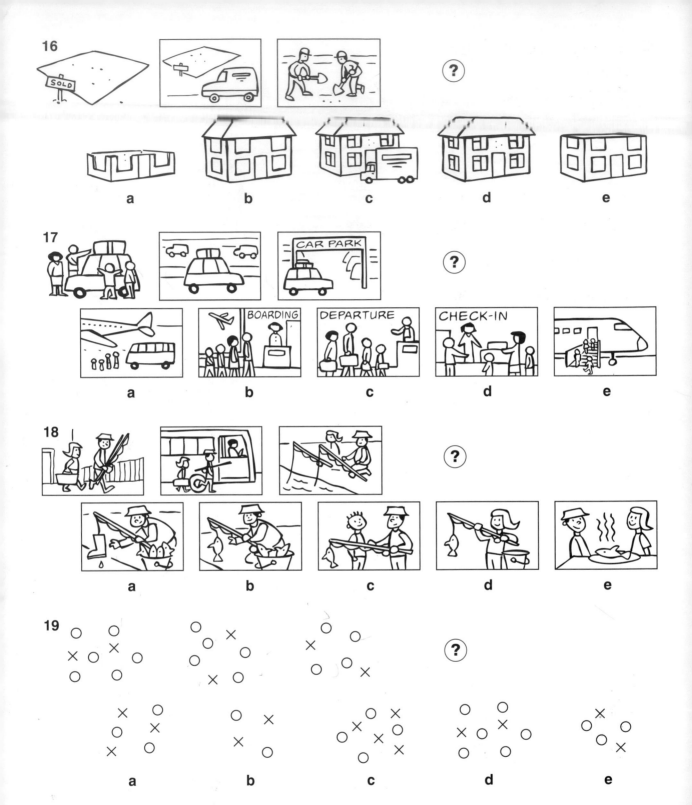

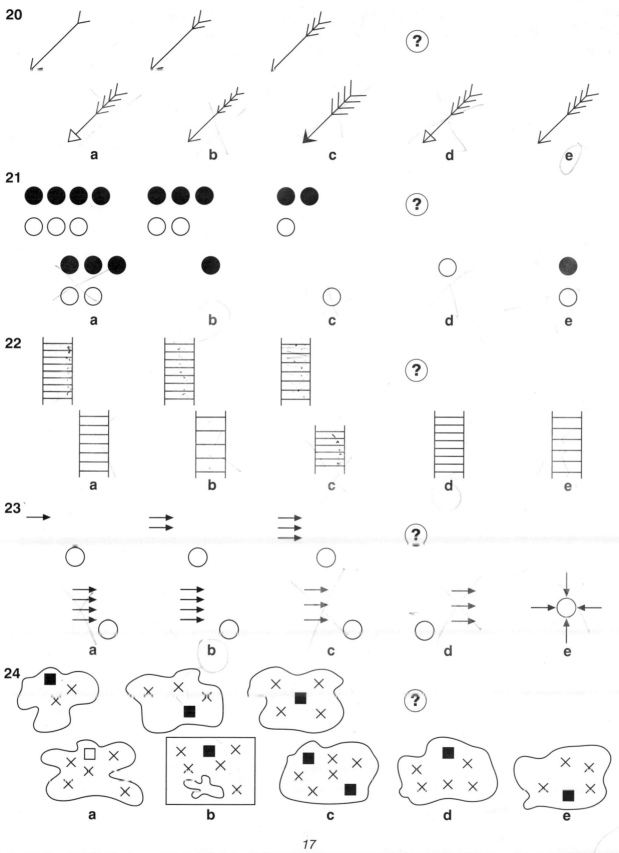

20

a b c d e

21

a b c d e

22

a b c d e

23

a b c d e

24

a b c d e

17

Choose the picture which completes the second pair in the same way as the first pair.
Circle the letter.

Example

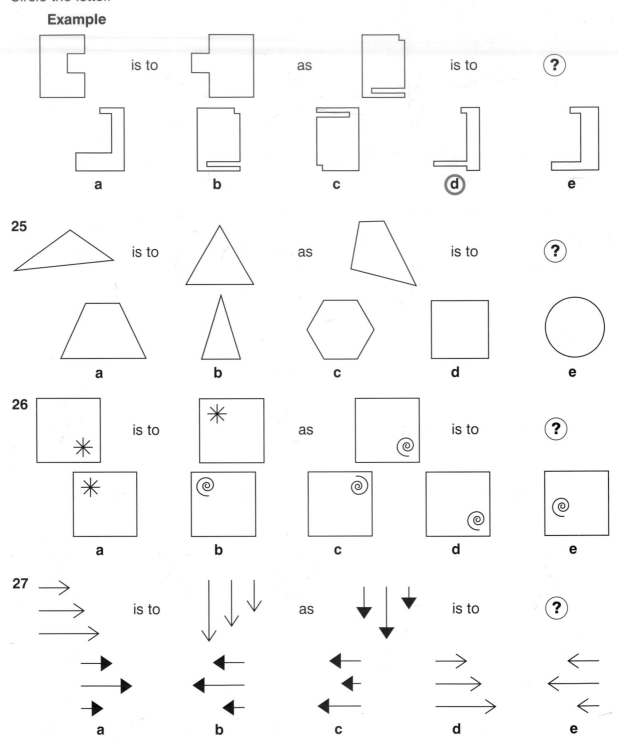

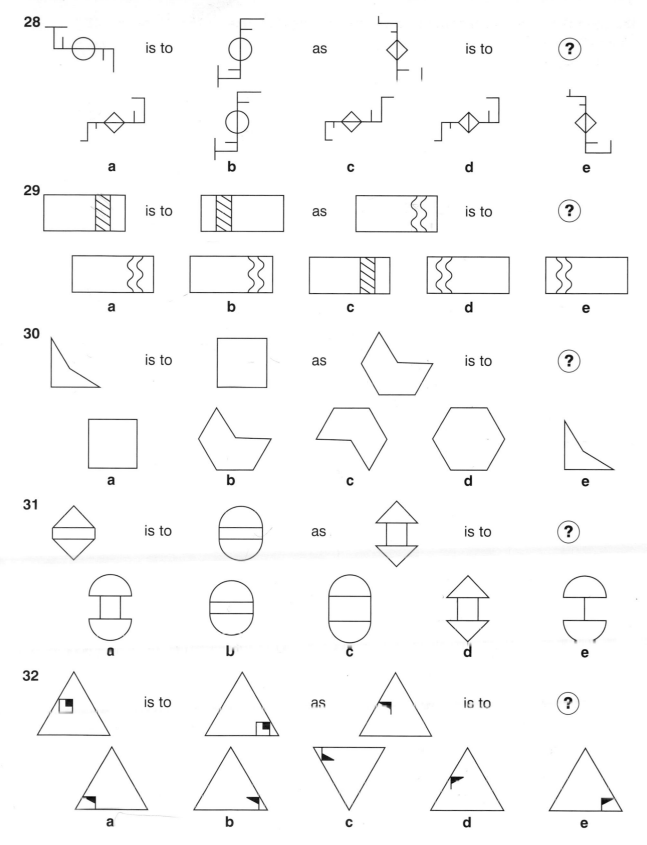

28

is to ... as ... is to ... ?

a   b   c   d   e

29

is to ... as ... is to ... ?

a   b   c   d   e

30

is to ... as ... is to ... ?

a   b   c   d   e

31

is to ... as ... is to ... ?

a   b   c   d   e

32

is to ... as ... is to ... ?

a   b   c   d   e

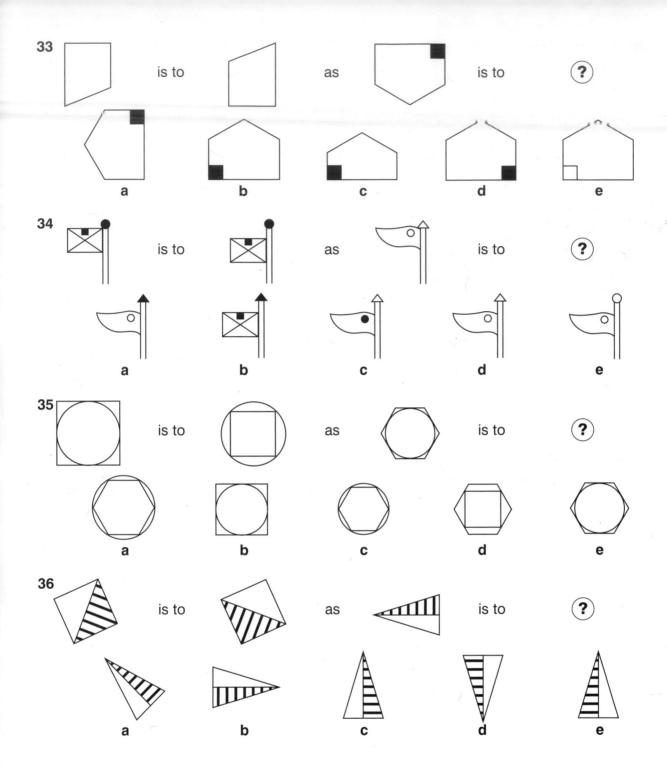

33

34

35

36

In which larger shape or pattern is the smaller shape hidden? Circle the letter.

Example

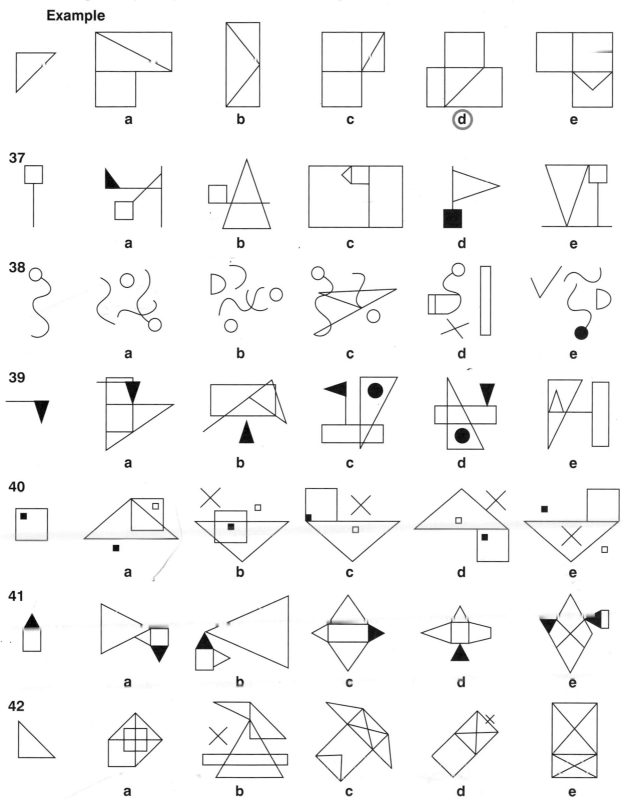

a b c d e

37 a b c d e

38 a b c d e

39 a b c d e

40 a b c d e

41 a b c d e

42 a b c d e

Which picture on the right is the reflection of the picture given on the left, in the dotted mirror line? Circle the letter.

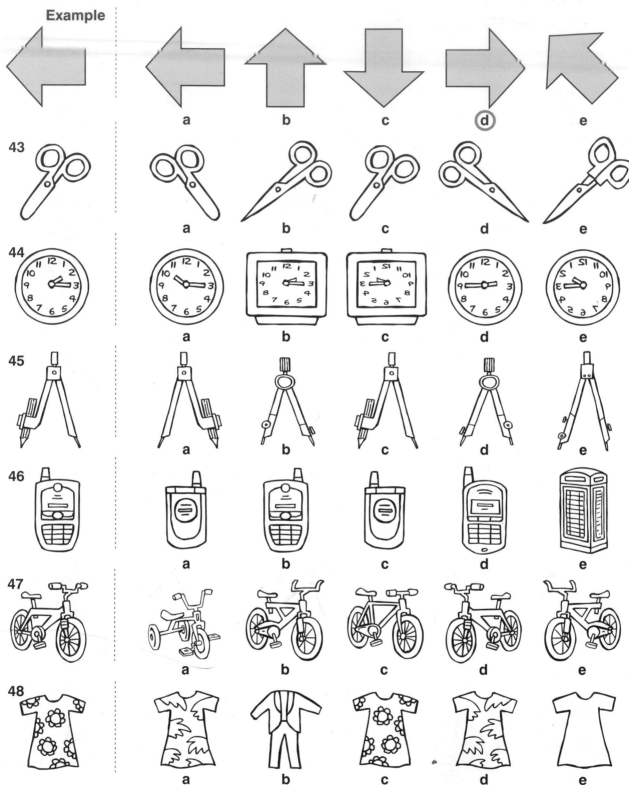

Example

a   b   c   d   e

43   a   b   c   d   e

44   a   b   c   d   e

45   a   b   c   d   e

46   a   b   c   d   e

47   a   b   c   d   e

48   a   b   c   d   e

Paper 3

Which is the odd one out? Circle the letter.

Example

a   b   ⓒ   d   e

1   a   b   c   d   e

2   a   b   c   d   e

3   a   b   c   d   e

4   a   b   c   d   e

5   a   b   c   d   e

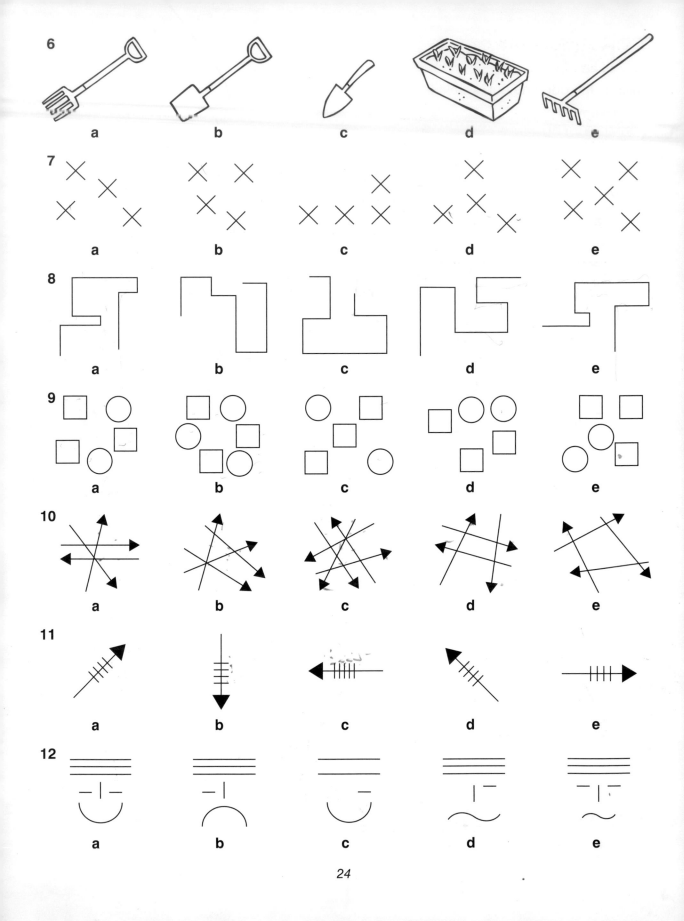

Which one comes next? Circle the letter.

Example

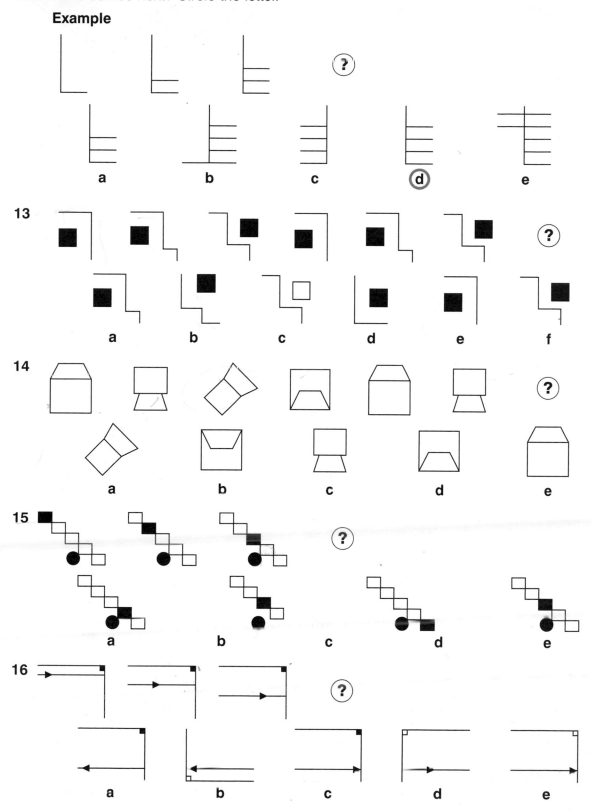

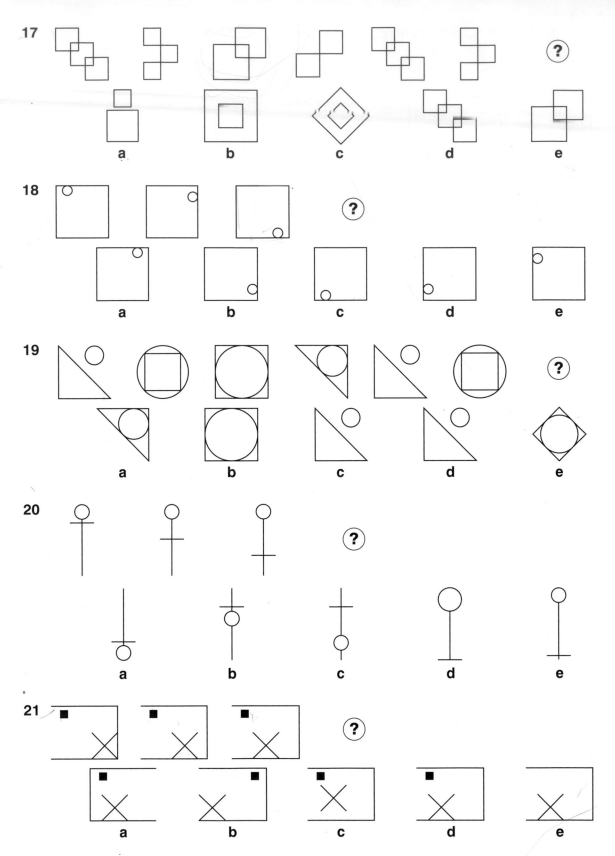

17

a   b   c   d   e

18

a   b   c   d   e

19

a   b   c   d   e

20

a   b   c   d   e

21

a   b   c   d   e

22

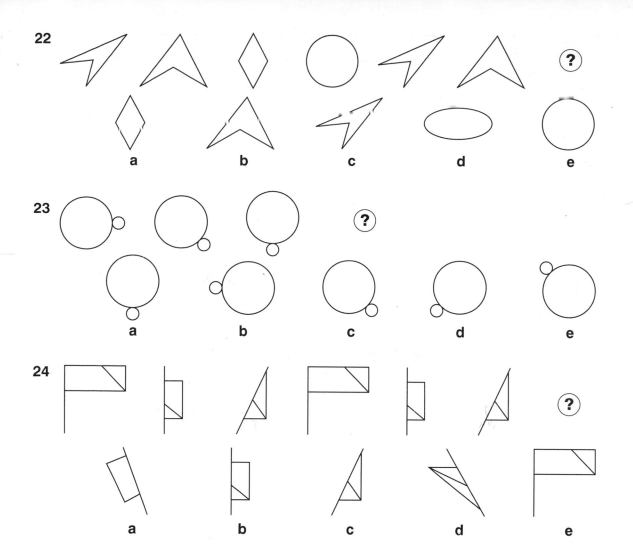

a b c d e

23

a b c d e

24

a b c d e

Choose the picture which completes the second pair in the same way as the first pair.
Circle the letter.

Example

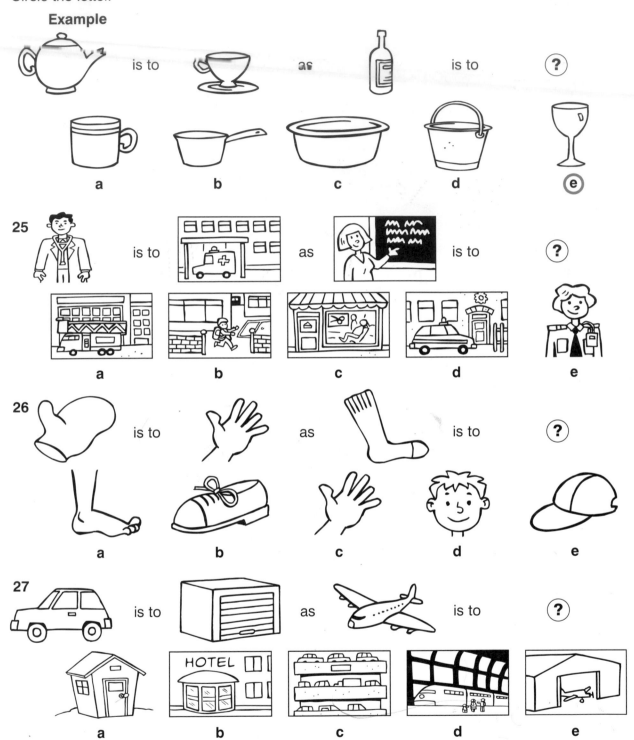

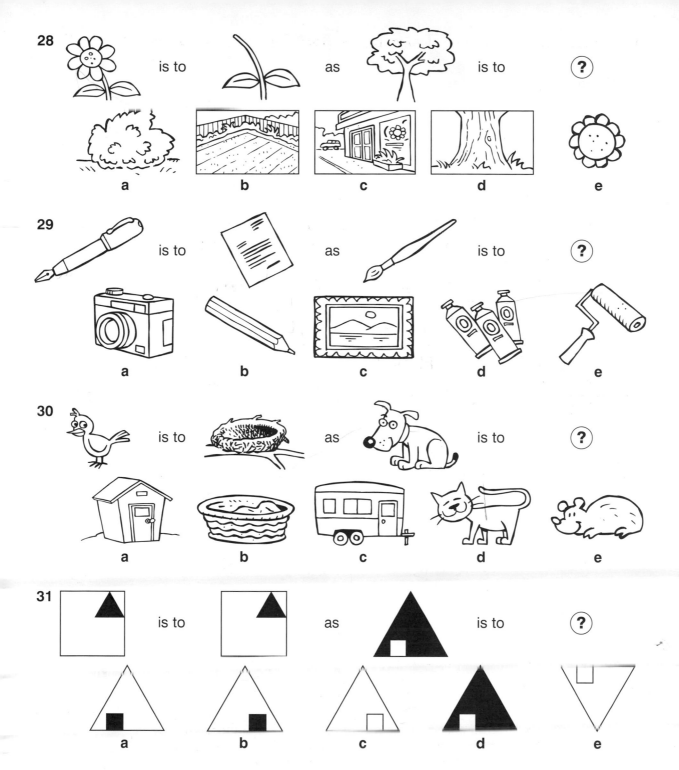

28

is to ... as ... is to ?

a   b   c   d   e

29

is to ... as ... is to ?

a   b   c   d   e

30

is to ... as ... is to ?

a   b   c   d   e

31

is to ... as ... is to ?

a   b   c   d   e

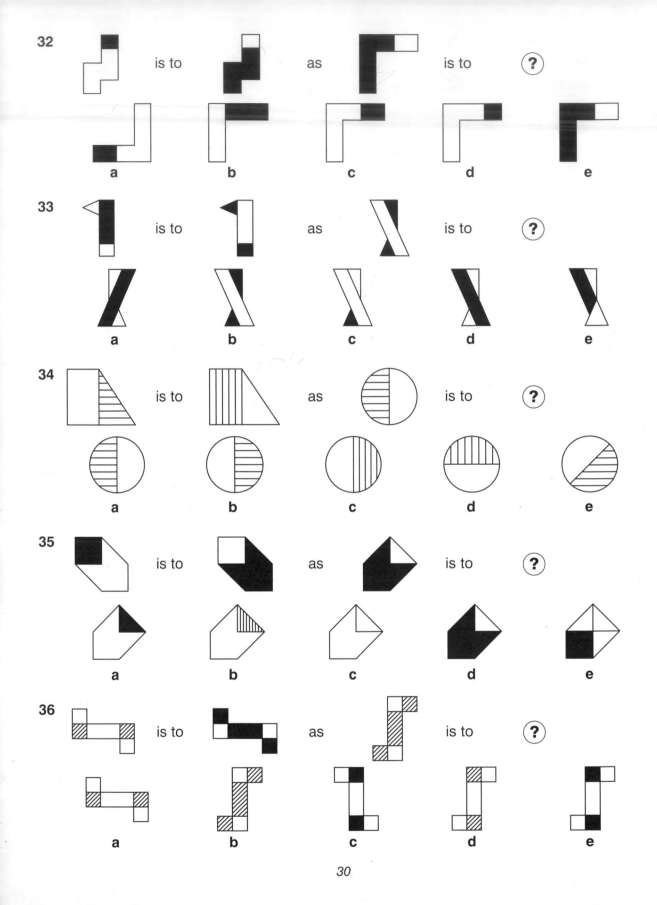

32   is to   as   is to   ?

a   b   c   d   e

33   is to   as   is to   ?

a   b   c   d   e

34   is to   as   is to   ?

a   b   c   d   e

35   is to   as   is to   ?

a   b   c   d   e

36   is to   as   is to   ?

a   b   c   d   e

Which shape on the right is the reflection of the shape given on the left, in the dotted mirror line? Circle the letter.

Example

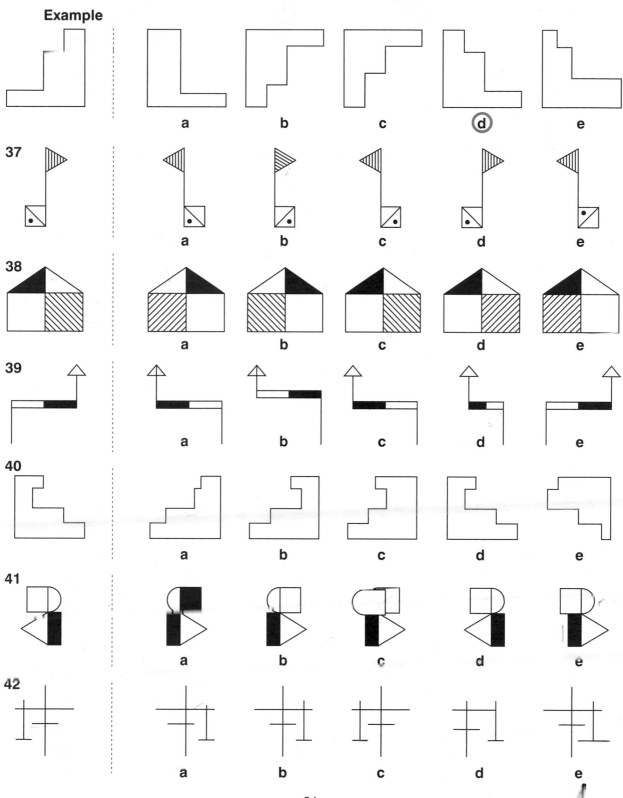

a   b   c   d   e

37   a   b   c   d   e

38   a   b   c   d   e

39   a   b   c   d   e

40   a   b   c   d   e

41   a   b   c   d   e

42   a   b   c   d   e

Choose the correct code for the picture given at the end of each line.

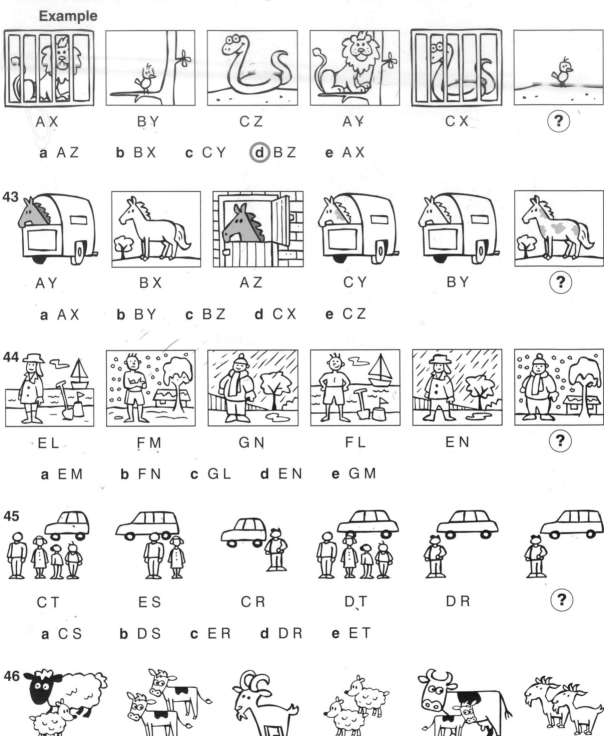

Example

AX   BY   CZ   AY   CX   ?

a AZ   **b** BX   **c** CY   **d** BZ   **e** AX

43

AY   BX   AZ   CY   BY   ?

a AX   **b** BY   **c** BZ   **d** CX   **e** CZ

44

EL   FM   GN   FL   EN   ?

a EM   **b** FN   **c** GL   **d** EN   **e** GM

45

CT   ES   CR   DT   DR   ?

a CS   **b** DS   **c** ER   **d** DR   **e** ET

46

RL   PK   QJ   RK   PL   ?

a RJ   **b** QL   **c** PJ   **d** PL   **e** QK

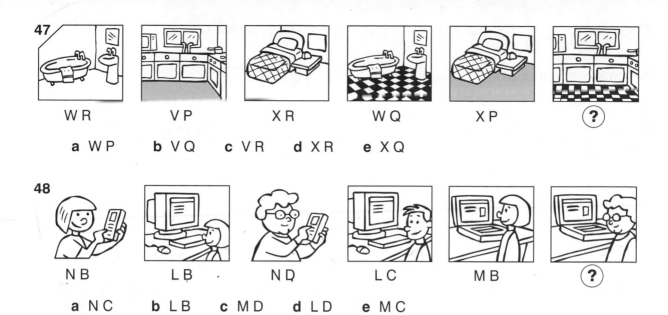

47

WR VP XR WQ XP **?**

a WP **b** VQ **c** VR **d** XR **e** XQ

48

NB LB ND LC MB **?**

a NC **b** LB **c** MD **d** LD **e** MC

Paper 4

Which is the odd one out? Circle the letter.

Example

a   b   c   d   e

1   a   b   c   d   e

2   a   b   c   d   e

3   a   b   c   d   e

4   a   b   c   d   e

5   a   b   c   d   e

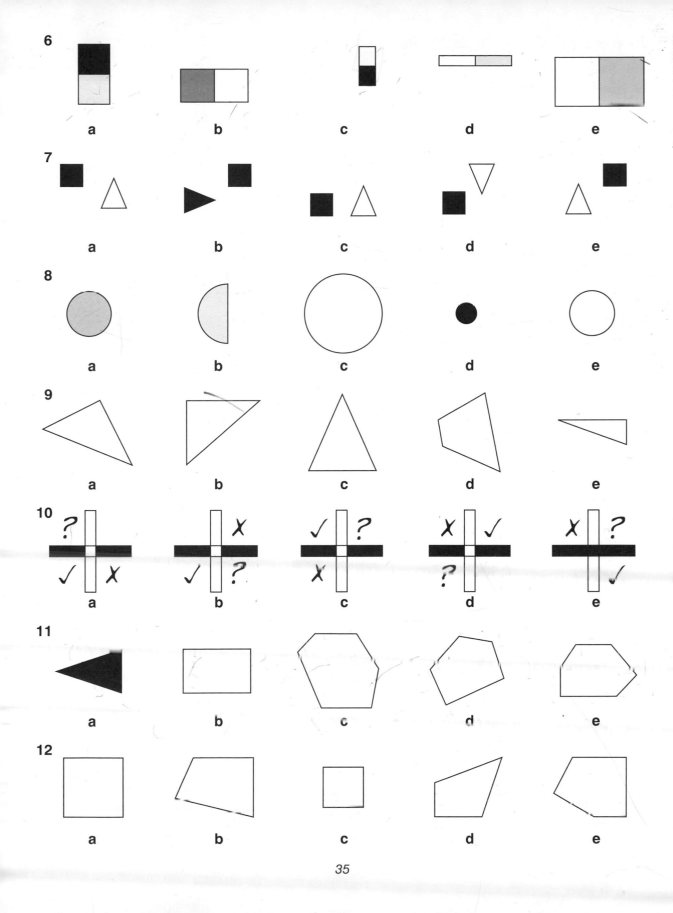

6

a b c d e

7

a b c d e

8

a b c d e

9

a b c d e

10

a b c d e

11

a b c d e

12

a b c d e

Which one comes next? Circle the letter.

Example

a   b   c   d   e

13

a   b   c   d   e

14

a   b   c   d   e

15

a   b   c   d   e

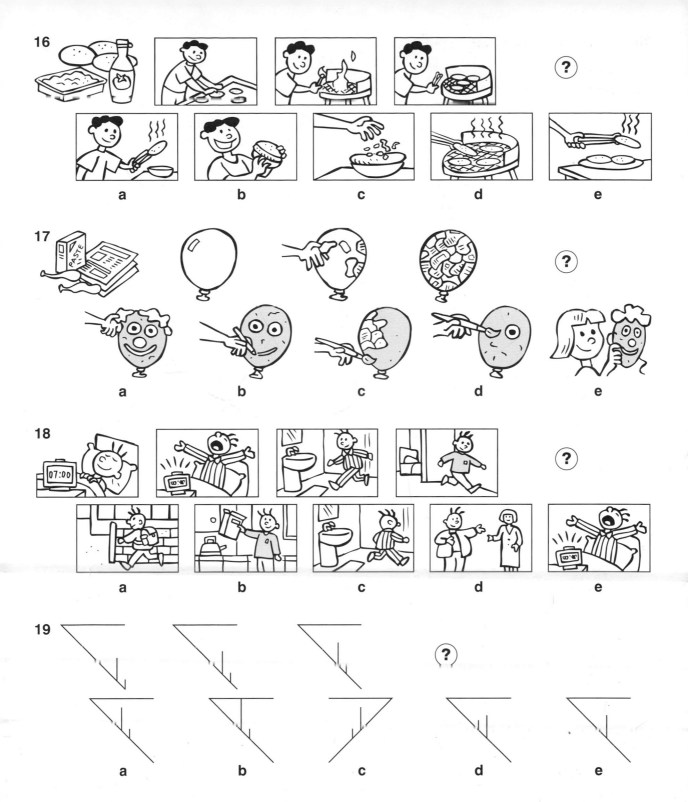

16   a   b   c   d   e

17   a   b   c   d   e

18   a   b   c   d   e

19   a   b   c   d   e

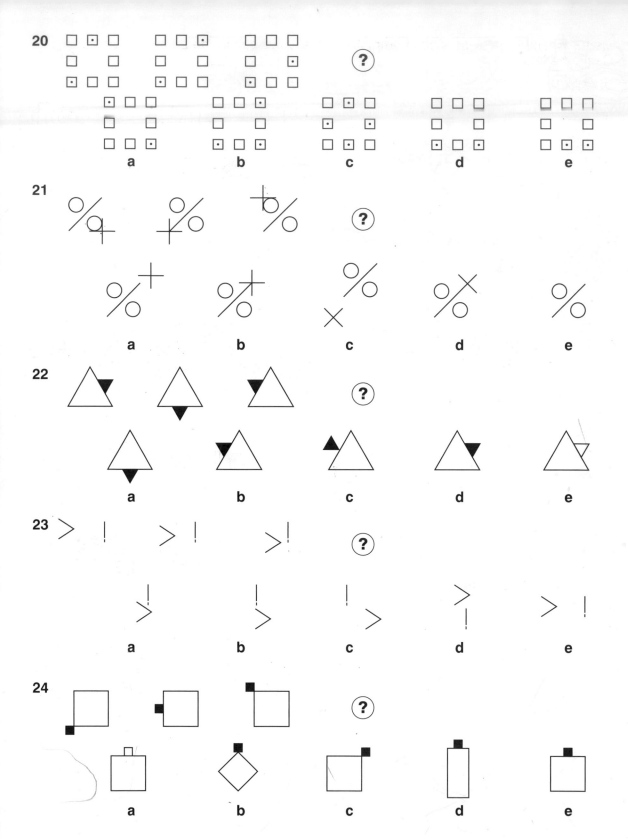

Choose the shape or pattern which completes the second pair in the same way as the first pair. Circle the letter.

Example

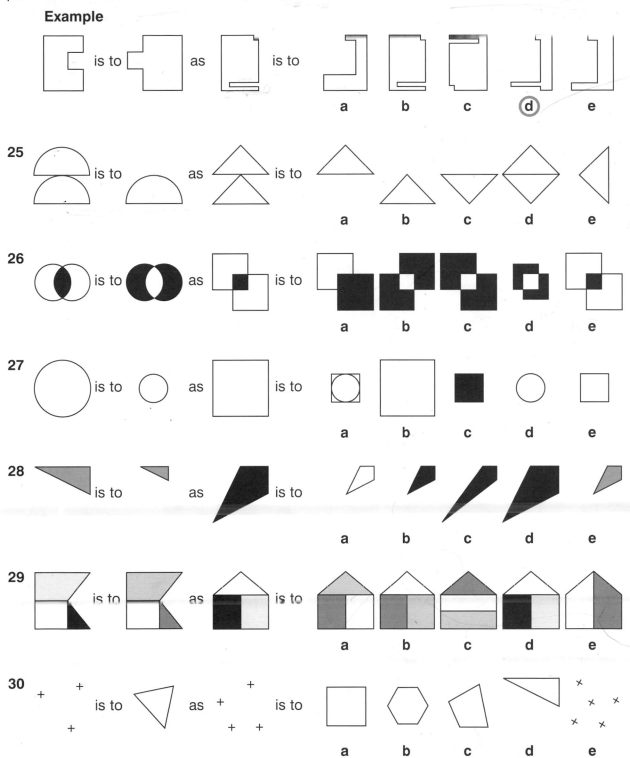

25

26

27

28

29

30

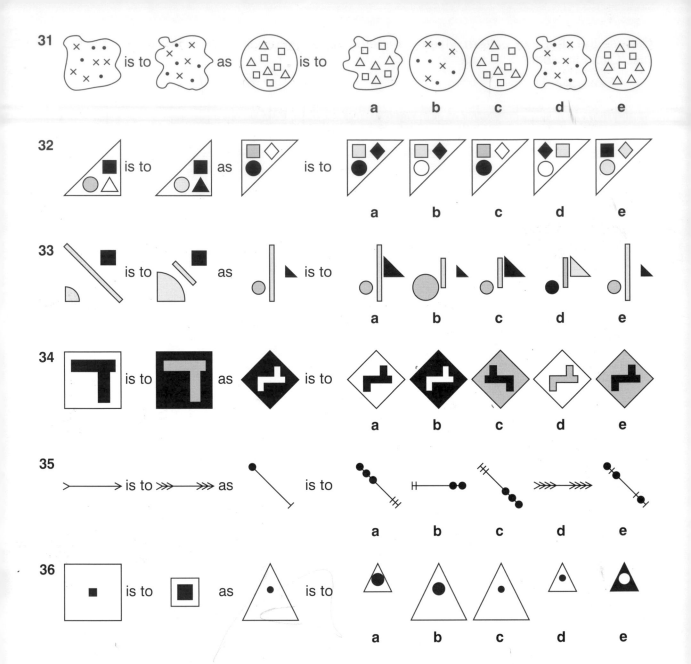

Choose the shape or pattern which completes the larger square. Circle the letter.

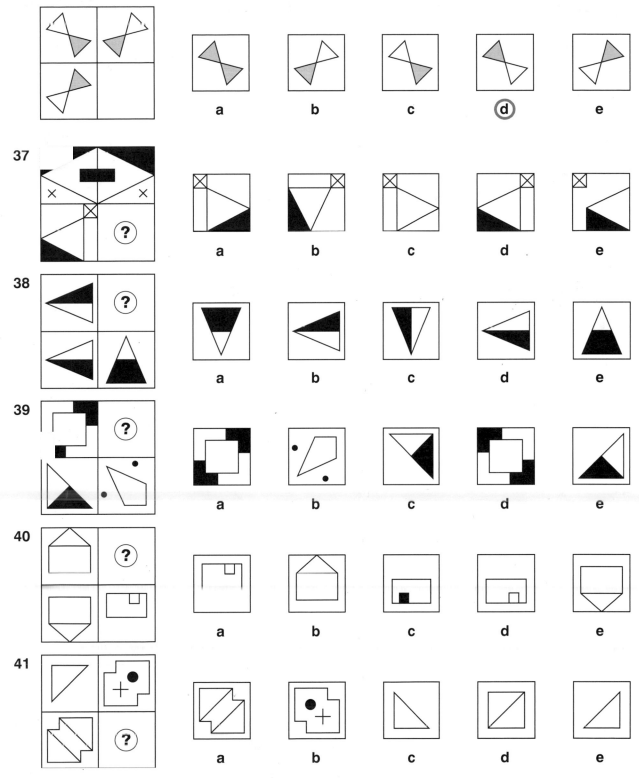

Example

a b c d e

37

a b c d e

38

a b c d e

39

a b c d e

40

a b c d e

41

a b c d e

42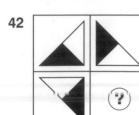

| | **a** | **b** | **c** | **d** | **e** |

Choose the correct code for the shape or pattern given at the end of each line.

Example

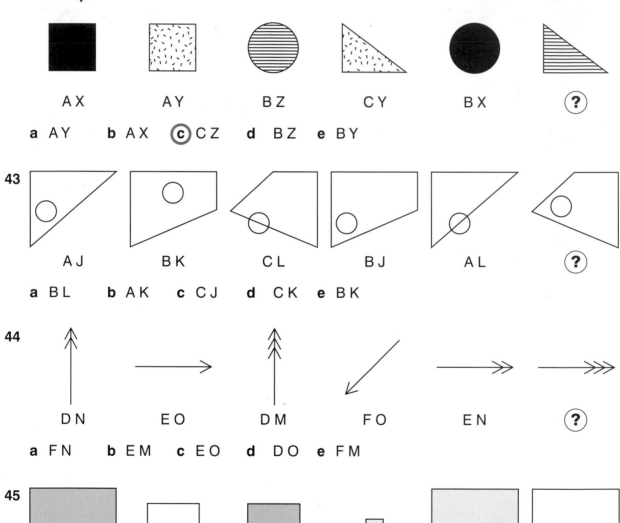

AX   AY   BZ   CY   BX   **?**

a AY   **b** AX   **c** CZ   **d** BZ   **e** BY

43

AJ   BK   CL   BJ   AL   **?**

a BL   **b** AK   **c** CJ   **d** CK   **e** BK

44

DN   EO   DM   FO   EN   **?**

a FN   **b** EM   **c** EO   **d** DO   **e** FM

45

FR   GS   GR   HT   FT   **?**

a GT   **b** HR   **c** HS   **d** FT   **e** FS

46

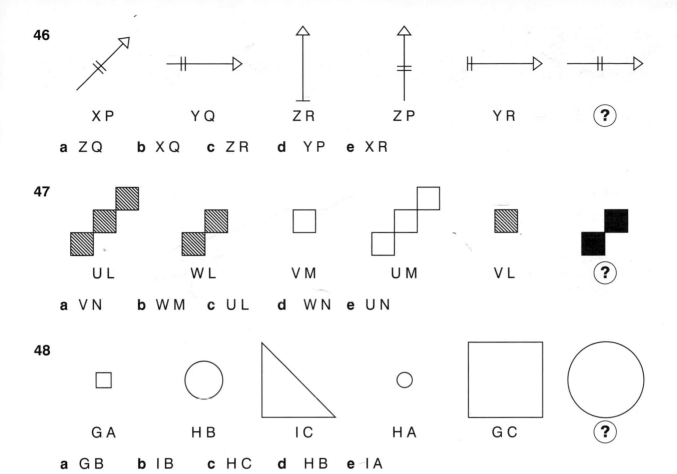

XP YQ ZR ZP YR (?)

a ZQ **b** XQ **c** ZR **d** YP **e** XR

47

UL WL VM UM VL (?)

a VN **b** WM **c** UL **d** WN **e** UN

48

GA HB IC HA GC (?)

a GB **b** IB **c** HC **d** HB **e** IA

Paper 5

Which is the odd one out? Circle the letter.

Example

a   b   ⓒ   d   e

1   a   b   c   d   e

2   a   b   c   d   e

3   a   b   c   d   e

4   a   b   c   d   e

5   a   b   c   d   e

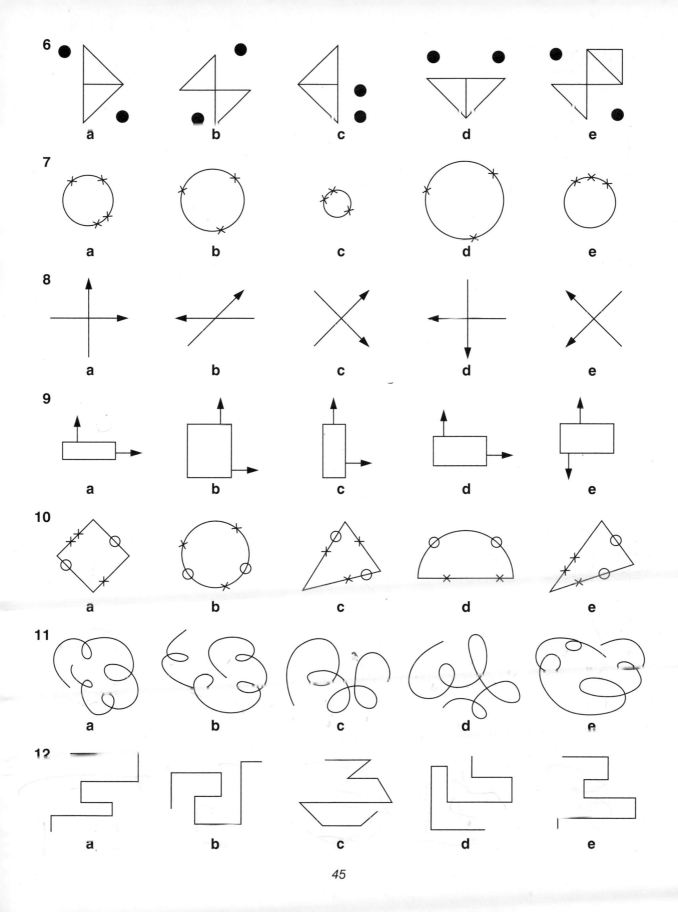

Which one comes next? Circle the letter.

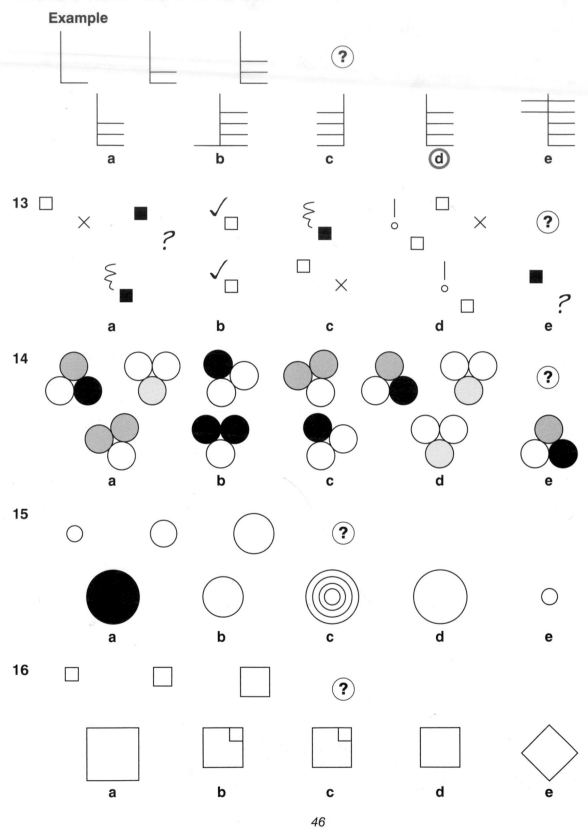

Example

13

14

15

16

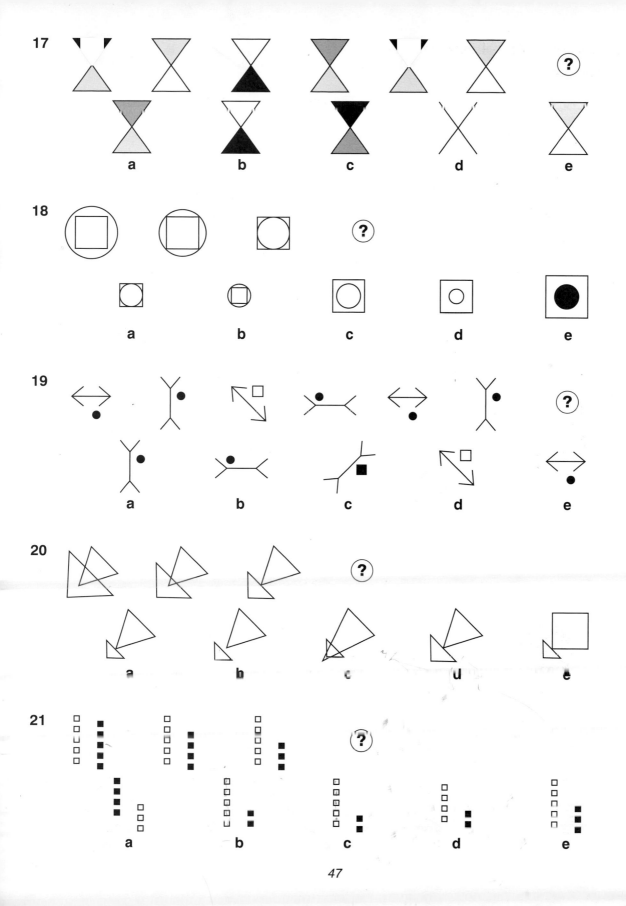

17

a b c d e

18

a b c d e

19

a b c d e

20

a b c u e

21

a b c d e

47

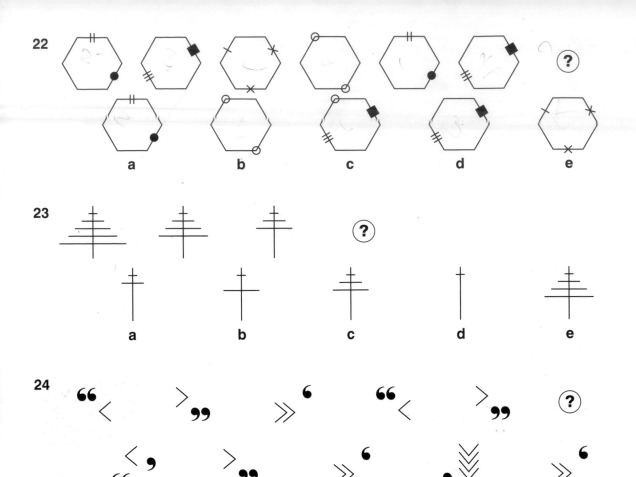

48

Choose the picture which completes the second pair in the same way as the first pair.
Circle the letter.

Example

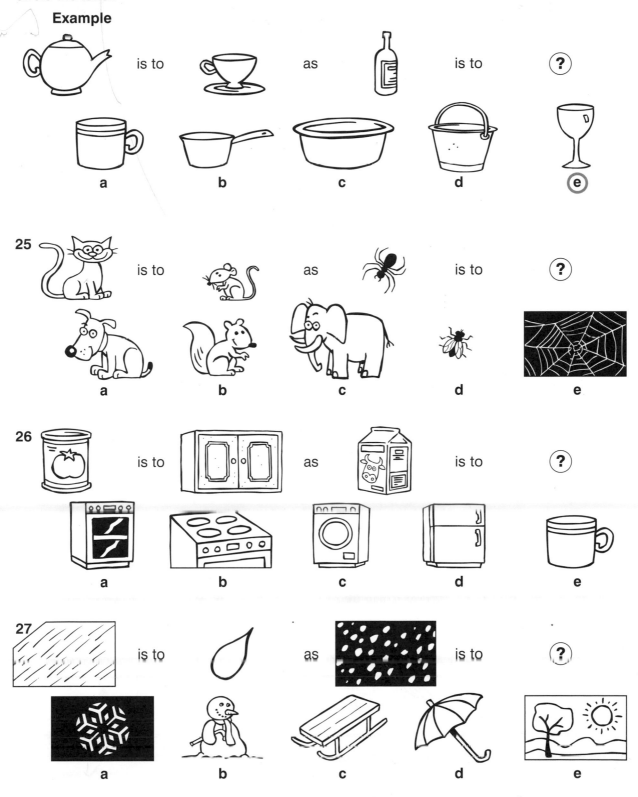

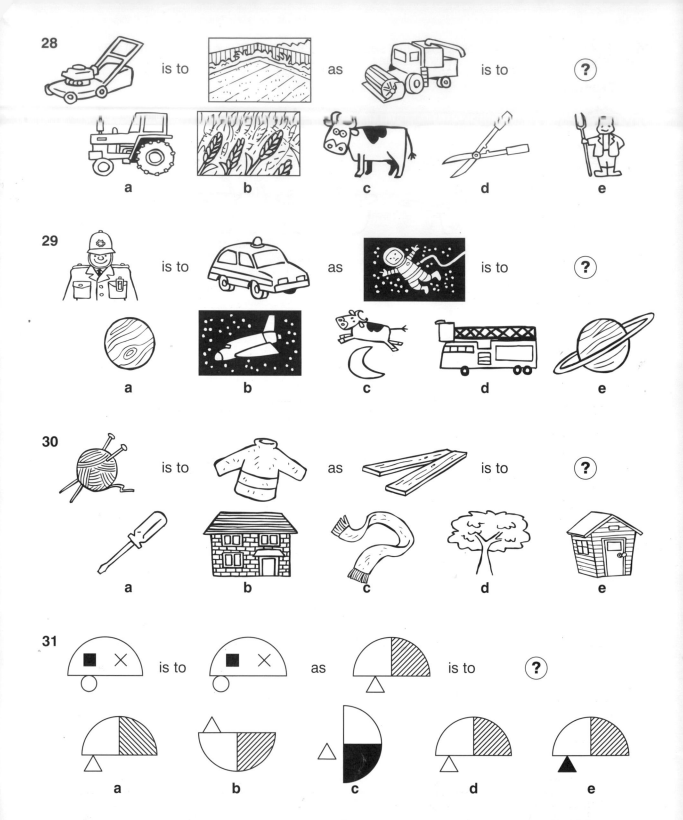

28 is to ... as ... is to **?**

a b c d e

29 is to ... as ... is to **?**

a b c d e

30 is to ... as ... is to **?**

a b c d e

31 is to ... as ... is to **?**

a b c d e

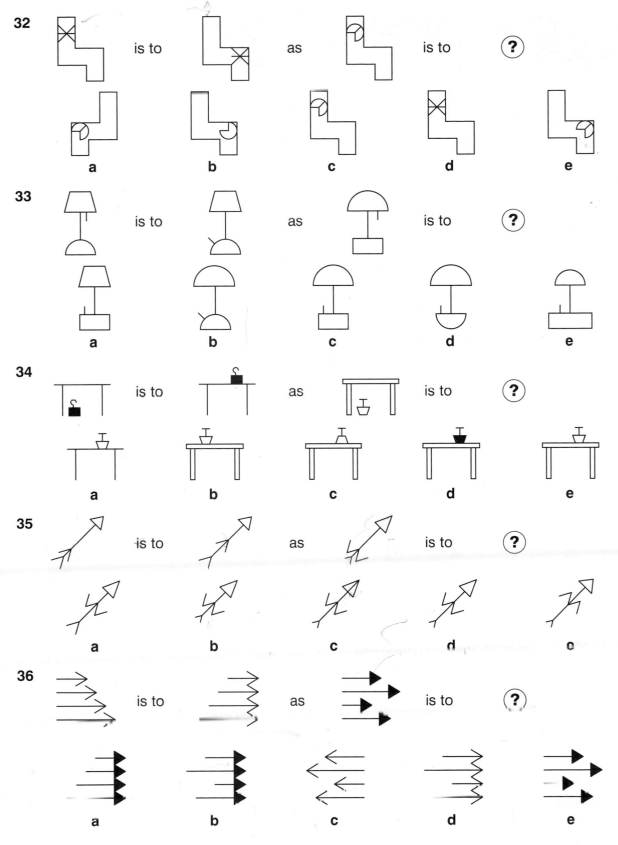

In which larger shape or pattern is the smaller shape hidden? Circle the letter.

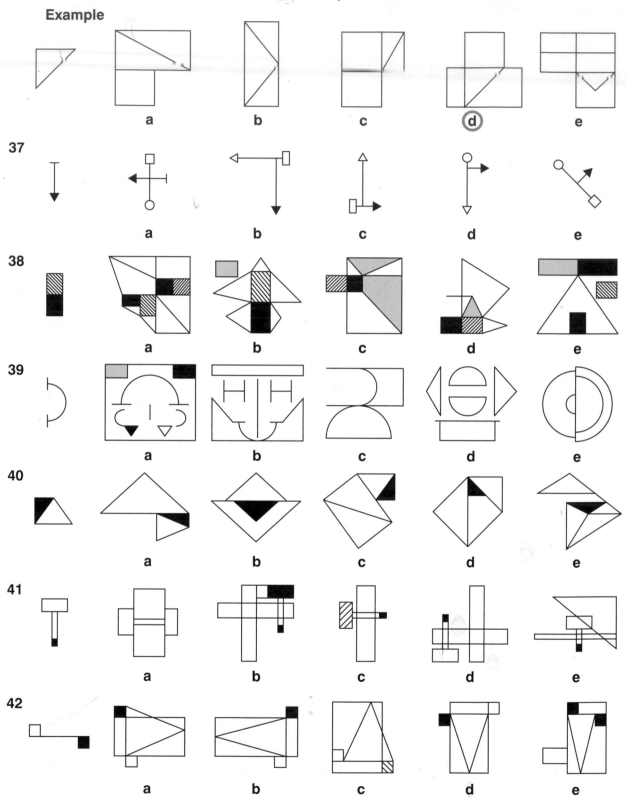

Example

a   b   c   (d)   e

37   a   b   c   d   e

38   a   b   c   d   e

39   a   b   c   d   e

40   a   b   c   d   e

41   a   b   c   d   e

42   a   b   c   d   e

Which shape on the right is the reflection of the shape given on the left, in the dotted mirror line? Circle the letter.

Example

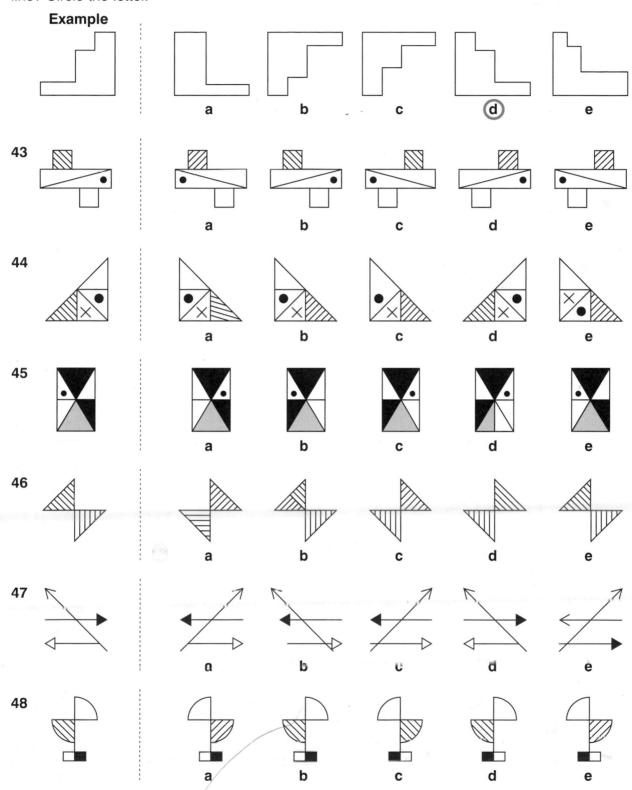

Paper 6

Which is the odd one out? Circle the letter.

Example

54

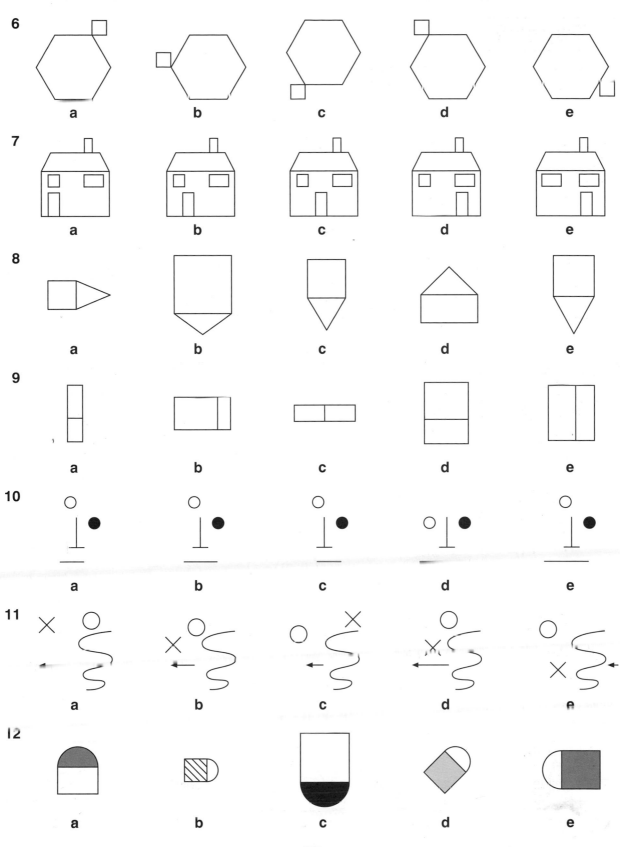

6

a   b   c   d   e

7

a   b   c   d   e

8

a   b   c   d   e

9

a   b   c   d   e

10

a   b   c   d   e

11

a   b   c   d   e

12

a   b   c   d   e

Which one comes next? Circle the letter.

Example

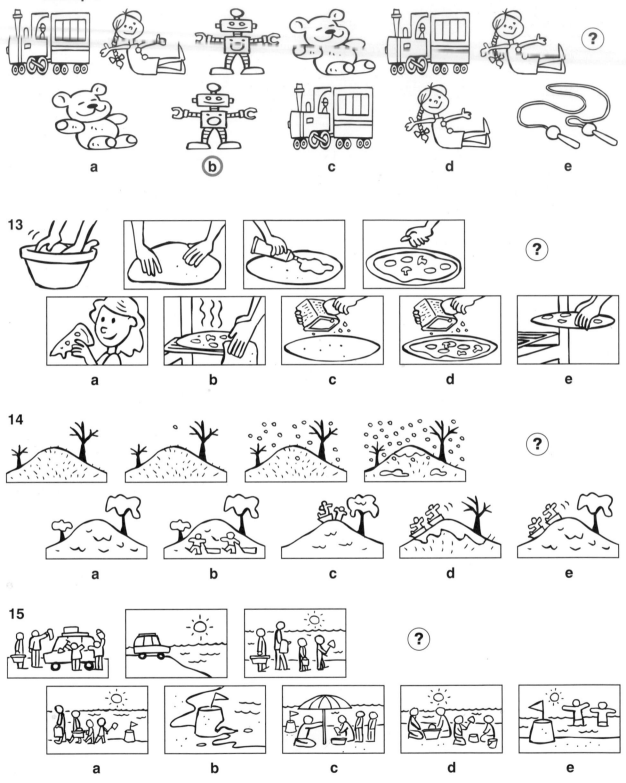

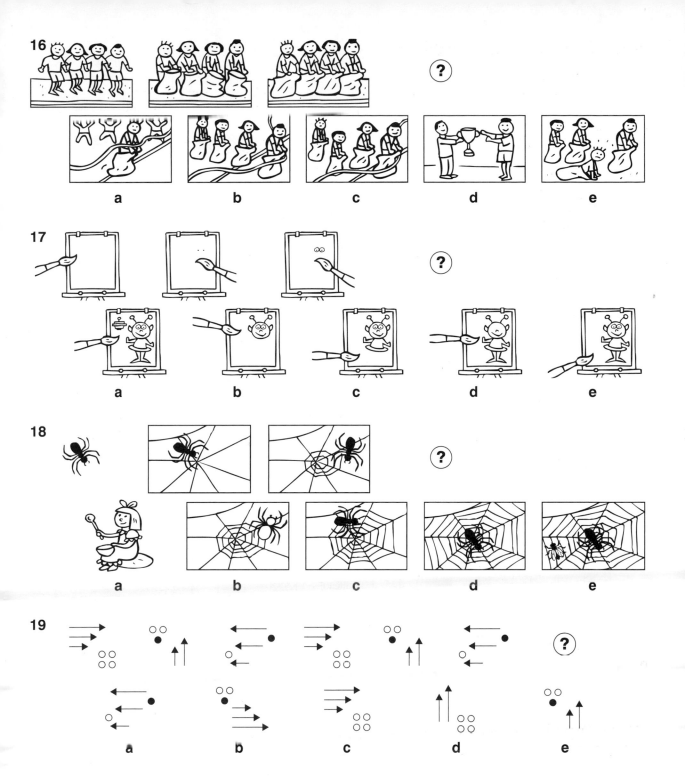

16

a b c d e

17

a b c d e

18

a b c d e

19

a b c d e

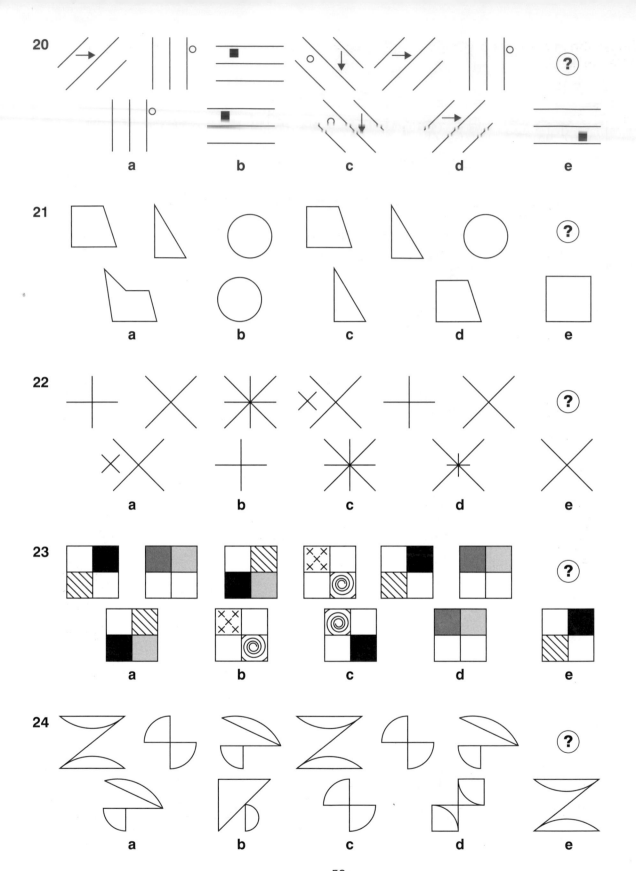

20

21

22

23

24

Choose the picture which completes the second pair in the same way as the first pair.
Circle the letter.

Example

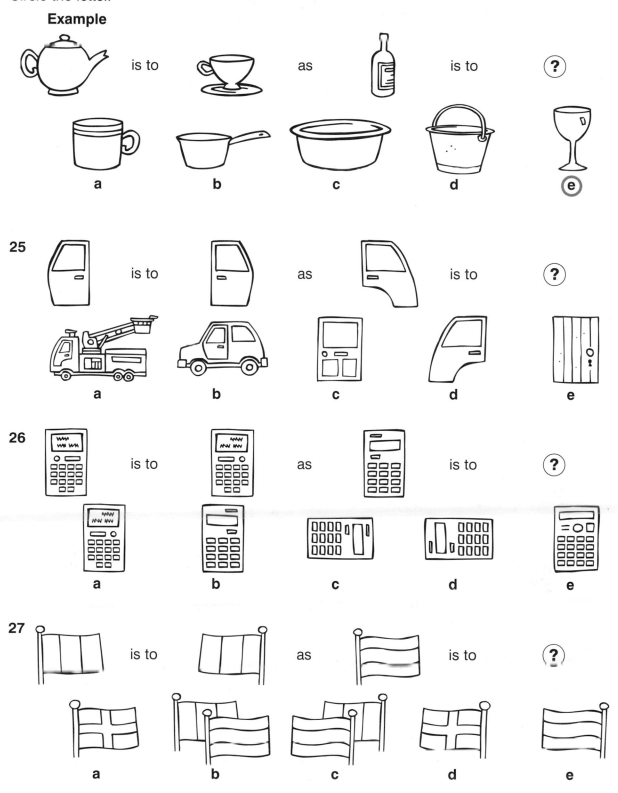

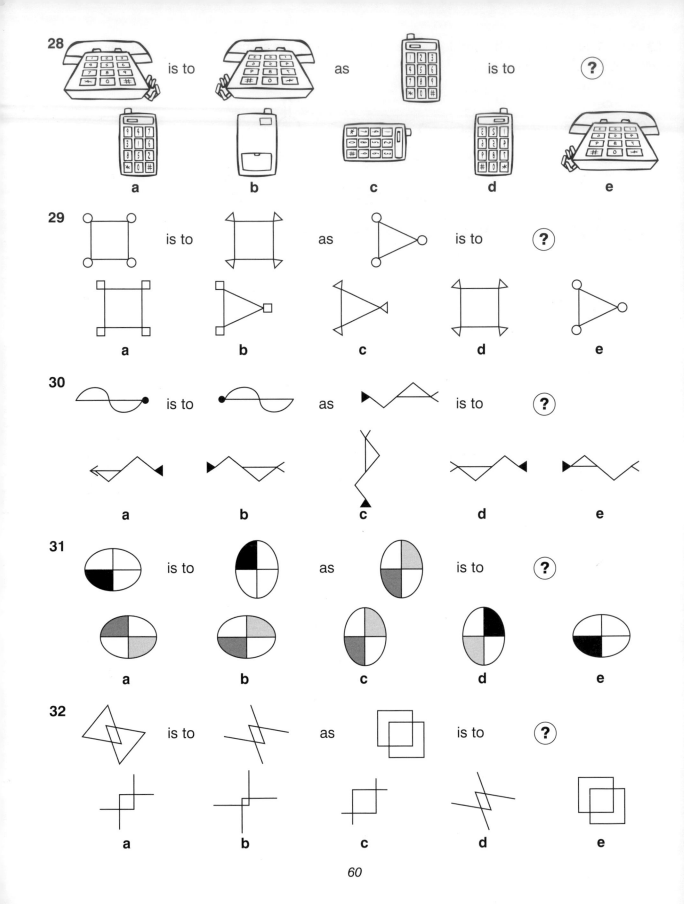

28

29

30

31

32

60

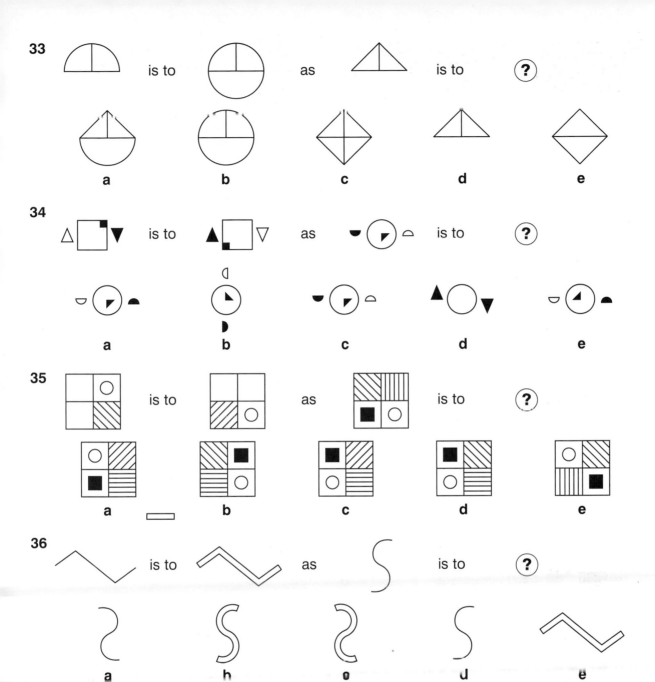

33

a   **b**   **c**   **d**   **e**

34

a   **b**   **c**   **d**   **e**

35

a   **b**   **c**   **d**   **e**

36

a   **b**   **c**   **d**   **e**

Choose the shape or pattern which completes the larger square. Circle the letter.

Example

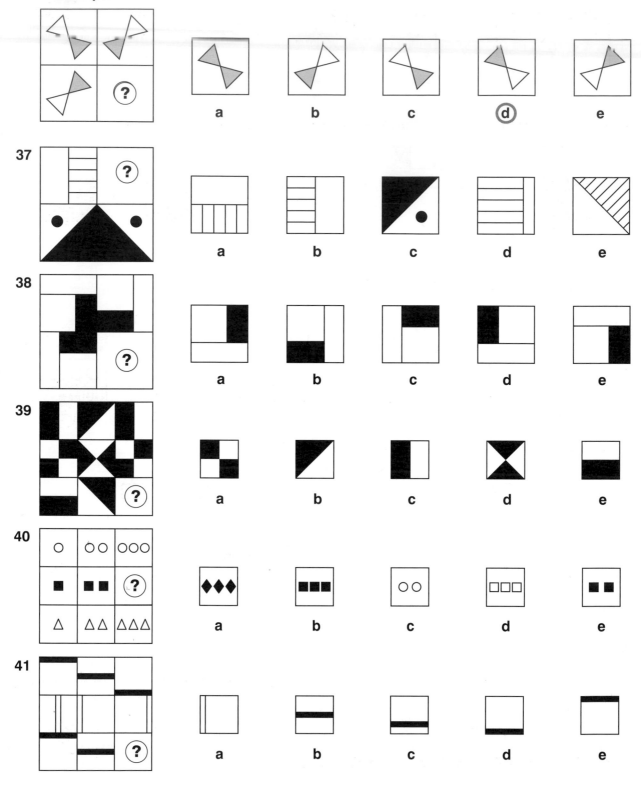

42

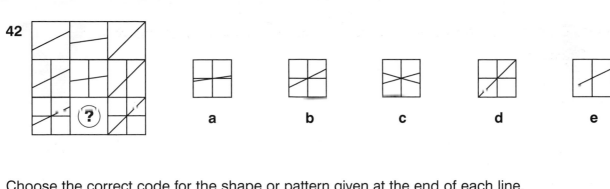

Choose the correct code for the shape or pattern given at the end of each line.

Example

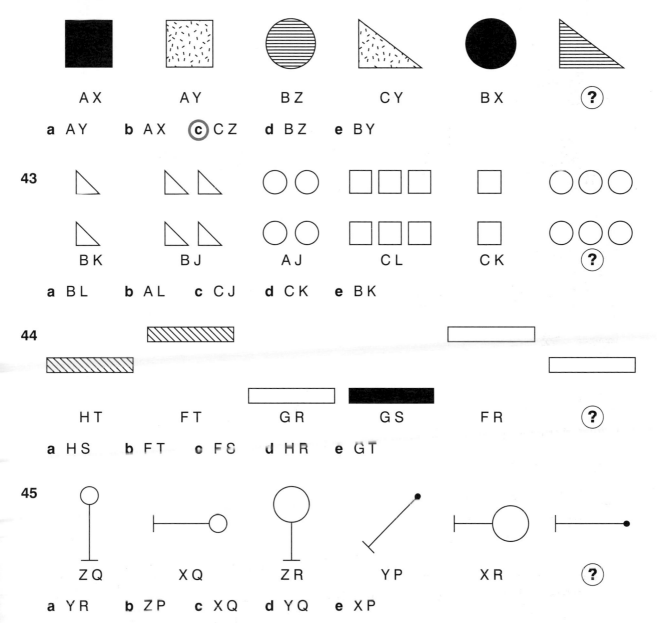

AX AY BZ CY BX **?**

a AY **b** AX **ⓒ** CZ **d** BZ **e** BY

43

BK BJ AJ CL CK **?**

a BL **b** AL **c** CJ **d** CK **e** BK

44

HT FT GR GS FR **?**

a HS **b** FT **c** FS **d** HR **e** GT

45

ZQ XQ ZR YP XR **?**

a YR **b** ZP **c** XQ **d** YQ **e** XP

46

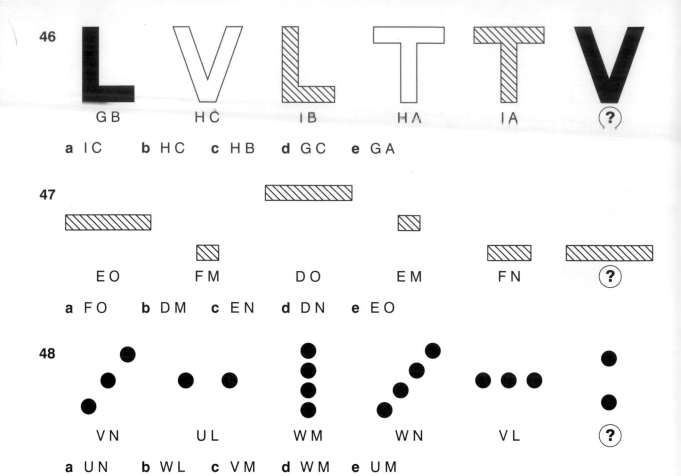

L V L T T V
GB HC IB HA IA (?)

a IC **b** HC **c** HB **d** GC **e** GA

47

EO FM DO EM FN (?)

a FO **b** DM **c** EN **d** DN **e** EO

48

VN UL WM WN VL (?)

a UN **b** WL **c** VM **d** WM **e** UM

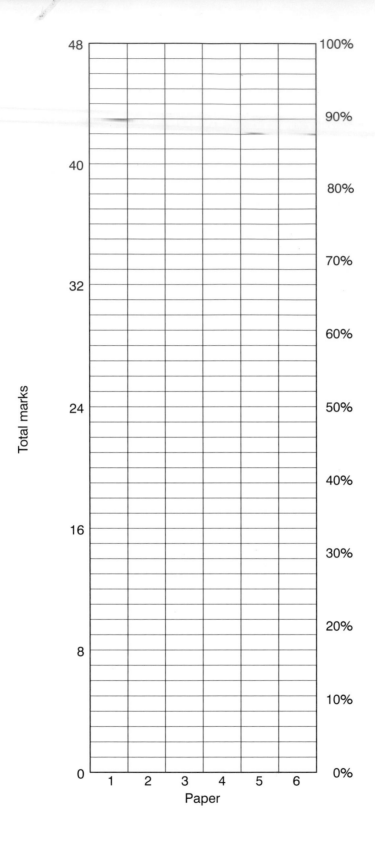